Zarbo®
ZEST

A catalogue record for this book is
available from the National Library of
New Zealand

A RANDOM HOUSE BOOK
published by
Random House New Zealand
18 Poland Road, Glenfield, Auckland,
New Zealand

www.randomhouse.co.nz

First published 2005. Reprinted 2006
Text © 2005 Mark McDonough
Photographs © 2005 Mark McDonough
and Random House New Zealand

The moral rights of the author have
been asserted

ISBN-10: 1 86941 628 7
ISBN-13: 978 1 86941 628 7

Photography: Donna North
Design: Trevor Newman

Printed in China

Zarbo®

ZEST

Mark McDonough

RANDOM HOUSE
NEW ZEALAND

contents

The release of this book coincides with Zarbo's tenth birthday, and what an amazing decade it has been. Our success is due to two things. First, the original partners had a clear vision — our classic look and expansive format have enabled us to age well and avoid the pitfall of being hot one day and not the next.

Second, I believe that it is our innovation and adaptation that have enabled us to lead the market for the past 10 years. In saying this, I must also acknowledge the support of our loyal community of staff and customers in building this success.

introduction

You will notice that this, the third book from Zarbo, has a new focus. For the first time I have included a selection of breakfast and brunch foods and there are chapters of café treats and deli delights. To help with meal planning there is a chapter featuring salads and another of mains that require a bit more effort, but you will be well rewarded for it. I feel sure the sweets will all become firm favourites. Dotted throughout you will find selections of 'flavour enhancers' — salsas, dressings and sauces. These are great for enlivening most meals. I find them especially useful to have on hand on week nights, when there's not a lot of time for meal preparation.

I have also included some traditional food-preserving techniques — smoking, bottling and jam-making. When I was a child, my mother would spend days slaving in the kitchen to preserve summer produce, while my father smoked eel and fresh trout from his many fishing trips. I am one of 10 children, so I am sure you can imagine the volumes of food they preserved. These skills are far too important to lose. There is nothing more satisfying than getting back to basics, taking tradition and re-working it with new ingredients.

I like to be creative and I like to adapt and use a variety of products, often challenging traditional ideas, and I encourage you all to do the same. I try not to be too exclusive in selecting ingredients. With this in mind, when testing these recipes I have purchased most of the ingredients from my local supermarket and Asian food market — there are only a few items that you will have to get from speciality food stores.

It is also important that these recipes work in a domestic kitchen so I have tested each recipe at home. However, you may need to adjust the cooking temperatures and times to suit your oven.

I am lucky that my wife Cushla, before studying medicine, completed a degree in nutrition. She is always available to advise me on how to balance food and nutrients for our health and well-being. The *British Medical Journal* reported, in December 2004, that scientists believe they have discovered an eating plan that can cut heart disease by 76 per cent. They call this recipe for life 'the Polymeal'. The Polymeal consists of a diet that includes wine, dark chocolate, fruits and vegetables, almonds and garlic eaten on a daily basis, and fish four times a week. It's interesting that they put wine and dark chocolate first!

The main emphasis, however, is on fresh produce and I have always advocated choosing the best fresh produce available. Whenever possible I try to buy each day what I want to cook that night. I realise that this is not practical for many of us most of the time, but by making a few simple changes about how we purchase fresh produce we really can improve the quality of what we eat.

Having young children in the house has made the challenge of writing this book all the more rewarding. While Olive, who is 18 months old, has been pretty relaxed about the whole process, Felix, who is now four and a half, is keen to be my personal assistant. He has appointed himself 'Zarbo Junior Chef' and is working on his own cookbook — titled *Chuck Up* that includes recipes for rice cracker and sultana sandwiches and a very unusual frozen treat consisting of marmite and yoghurt. How's that for fusion?

As always there are people to thank. Thanks to Colin Thompson from the Zarbo Bakery for trialling a number of the sweet recipes. Donna North has, once again, done an amazing job — her food styling and photography are what make my books. Thanks to the team at Random House for their encouragement and support. To my sister, Diane Dolan, and all the loyal Zarbo staff, now and over the past decade, I am truly grateful. To all our customers, who over the years have helped build the strong community feeling, thank you for your support and encouragement. Saving the best for last, Cushla, Felix and Olive are always there for me at the end of each day, helping me maintain a positive work–life balance.

firstthing

firstthing

Breakfast is the most important meal of the day. However, if you are anything like me you find that the period between getting out of bed and leaving the house is not long enough to do all the things you need to do. That's one reason I like smoothies — they can be prepared the night before, made in the morning and any mess can go straight into the dishwasher and be forgotten about. Muesli is another great idea for our time-poor generation — a batch of muesli made in the weekend and kept in an airtight container will last all week.

I also like to make a few jams to have in the pantry when fruit is in season. The jam and marma-lade in this section offer new taste sensations. It is important to have a good work–life balance and for this reason I have included a couple of classic brunch dishes — the sort of thing I like to make in the weekends for friends, or when I just want to chill out with the Sunday paper.

Smoothies are a great way to start the day. Here are just two examples. Play around and come up with your own favourites. I recommend making smoothies as soon as you get up, before you have a shower, collect the paper or whatever else you do in the morning — allowing smoothies to sit for just a few minutes helps to bring out the flavours.

mango, lime and ginger smoothie

Serves 2

1 mango, peeled and sliced off its stone
   (or tinned mango)
1 teaspoon grated ginger
rind and juice of 1 lime
4–5 ice cubes
1 large teaspoon honey, more to taste
1 cup low-fat yoghurt

Blend mango, ginger and lime rind and juice
until reasonably smooth. Add ice cubes and blend.
   Add the honey and yoghurt and
blend to desired consistency.

I used to think that smoothies would be too much effort in the morning, but really they aren't. You can even prepare everything the night before, ready to blend in the morning and, afterwards, throw the blender (jug only) into the dishwasher.

chocolate, orange and almond smoothie

Serves 1

2–3 tablespoons grated dark chocolate
1 cup freshly squeezed orange juice
2 tablespoons toasted almonds
½ cup unsweetened low-fat yoghurt

Place all in a blender and blend to desired consistency.
    Note: You will need a spoon to stir the smoothie and to spoon out the chocolate and nuts.

I like to add the fruit immediately
after removing muesli from the oven
— it helps to release the sugars
from the fruit.

decadent toasted muesli

Makes approximately 12 cups

6 cups rolled oats
1 cup pumpkin kernels
1 cup cashew nuts, roughly chopped
⅓ cup grapeseed oil
¾ cups orange juice
1 teaspoon cinnamon
½ teaspoon grated fresh nutmeg
½ cup coconut thread
1 cup toasted hazelnuts, husks
   removed and roughly chopped
½ cup dried cranberries
½ cup dried nectarines, sliced
1 cup dried mango, sliced
½ cup dates, sliced
½ cup dried peaches, sliced

Set oven to 200ºC.
   Combine rolled oats, pumpkin kernels,
cashew nuts, oil, juice and spices and
spread in a roasting dish. Bake for
10 to 15 minutes until golden. Stir a few
times to ensure even baking. Add the
coconut and hazelnuts and return to
the oven for a further 5 minutes.
Stir fruit through and allow to cool.
   Stored in an airtight container it
will keep for up to two weeks.

rolled oats with rhubarb compote

Serves 4

350g rolled oats
400ml cold water
½ teaspoon salt
500ml milk
450g rhubarb, trimmed
2 tablespoons balsamic vinegar
350g caster sugar
45ml water

To prepare the rolled oats, combine the oats, water and salt in a heavy-based saucepan. Place over heat and stir in the milk. Bring to the boil, reduce heat and simmer until oats are tender, approximately 8 to10 minutes.

   To prepare the rhubarb compote, slice the rhubarb and place in a heavy-based saucepan with the vinegar, sugar and water. Cook until the rhubarb is tender and the liquid reduced. Serve on top of rolled oats.

To test jams, jellies and marmalades for setting point, put a little of the hot liquid on a cold plate. Leave to cool slightly and if the surface wrinkles when touched and a channel formed by drawing a finger through remains open, the mixture will set.

strawberry balsamic jam

Makes approximately 6 cups

1kg strawberries, washed, tops removed
900g sugar
3 tablespoons lemon juice
3 tablespoons balsamic vinegar

Place strawberries and sugar in a non-reactive saucepan. Combine, cover and stand for a few hours.

Add lemon juice and balsamic vinegar and bring to the boil. Boil 15 to 20 minutes until setting point is reached. Allow to stand for 10 minutes and pour into sterilised jars.

lime and kaffir lime leaf marmalade

Makes approximately 6 cups

1kg limes, rinsed in cold water and soaked overnight
water (to soak limes)
4 large kaffir lime leaves, whole
4 cups caster sugar, heated
6–8 kaffir lime leaves, finely sliced

Slice the limes thinly and place in a non-reactive bowl. Add enough cold water to just cover the sliced limes. Stand overnight. Next day, transfer to a non-reactive saucepan along with the whole lime leaves. Bring to the boil, reduce heat and simmer for one hour or until the volume is reduced by about one-half.

Add sugar and stir until dissolved. Boil until setting point is reached, stirring occasionally. When setting point has been reached fold through the sliced lime leaves and pour into sterilised jars.

Fritters are a nice idea for brunch. With the addition of coconut milk these have a nice tropical flavour. Serve either with grilled bacon and sweet chilli sauce (page 73), or with tropical fruits and maple syrup.

kumara and coconut fritters

Serves 4

2 cups flour
2 teaspoons baking powder
½ teaspoon five spice
2 eggs
1 cup coconut cream
250g golden kumara, peeled, cooked and mashed
salt and pepper to taste
1 medium onion, finely diced
1 tomato, seeds removed and finely chopped
½ cup corn kernels
oil for frying

In a bowl, mix the flour, baking powder and five spice. In a second bowl, beat the eggs and the coconut cream and add the mashed kumara. Season with salt and pepper.

Add the egg mix to the dry ingredients. If the mixture is too wet add more flour. Add the onion, tomato and corn.

In a heavy-based frying pan, heat a little oil and drop tablespoons of batter onto the pan and brown. Flip and brown the reverse side.

Here's another great idea for brunch. Harissa is a spicy, Moroccan chilli paste. In this dish you only want a little bit to give a hint of heat — you don't want to overpower the other flavours.

potato harissa mash with bacon and poached eggs

Serves 4

1kg gourmet potatoes, cut into halves
1 teaspoon harissa paste, vary according to taste
⅓ cup olive oil
salt and pepper to taste
6–8 rashers lean bacon
8 eggs

Set oven to 170°C.
   Place the potatoes on a baking tray and coat with the harissa, oil, salt and pepper.
   Bake for 20 to 25 minutes until well cooked. While the potatoes are cooking, fry the bacon in a non-stick pan and poach the eggs.
   Roughly mash the cooked potatoes and divide between four plates. Top with the bacon and poached eggs.

This is a classic deli dish — ideal as a side dish, but equally comfortable as a brunch dish. Serve with crusty bread to soak up all the juices.

roasted field mushrooms

If mushrooms are extra large this will serve 6, if not it will serve 4

12 large Portobello mushrooms, brush top sides to remove any excess dirt
2 cloves garlic, finely diced
2 tablespoons balsamic vinegar
4 sage leaves, sliced
1 large sprig rosemary, pulled from the stalk
½ cup olive oil
sprigs of thyme
sea salt

Set oven to 160°C.
   Lay the mushrooms on a baking tray. Mix together garlic, vinegar, sage, rosemary and oil and brush over the mushrooms. Place sprigs of thyme on top and sprinkle with sea salt. Bake for 20 minutes.

cafétreats

café**treats**

New Zealanders have really embraced the café lifestyle. Our cities and towns are now brimming

with choice — we must have one of the highest numbers of cafés per head of population in the

world. In my travels I visit a lot of different cafés and I'm always inspired by what I see. For example,

Katz in New York has photos of the owners with each American president going back to the 1930s.

Here I have included variations of foods that you might see in a place like Katz: sauerkraut for a

Ruben sandwich and a traditional chicken soup. In cities like Rome, where you stand at the counter

to order an espresso, you see simple foods, such as the bruschetta pomodoro.

The salsas can be made in the weekend and stored in the fridge for use during the week. I like to

have a few of these on hand. Then I can simply pan-fry fish, or grill lamb, chicken or beef to serve

with either grilled vegetables or salad and rice or noodles. With the addition of a salsa, I have a

simple tasty meal in no time at all.

In this chapter there are also a couple of classics from the Zarbo kitchen that are guaranteed to

become firm family favourites. Many of these recipes are easy to adapt, so feel free to have a play.

Traditionally, sauerkraut is made by fermenting cabbage with kosher salt at room temperature for a period of 10 to12 days. However, this takes too long and daily attendance to remove scum is not that much fun. This cooked method is quicker and easier, and will keep for several weeks if refrigerated. It can also be frozen. For best results, make at least 24 hours in advance, refrigerate and allow the flavours to develop.

sauerkraut

Makes up to 2kg

1 large onion, peeled and finely sliced
3 cloves garlic, peeled and crushed
2 teaspoons caraway seeds
2 bay leaves
3 tablespoons olive oil
1 small head of cabbage, shredded
4 cups white wine
salt and pepper to taste
1 tablespoon honey
$\frac{1}{3}$ cup white wine vinegar

In a large heavy-based saucepan, sauté the onion, garlic, caraway seeds and bay leaves in a little oil until opaque. Add the cabbage and stir until well coated, approximately 4 to 5 minutes. Add the wine, seasoning, honey and vinegar. Cook uncovered for 45 minutes to one hour until well reduced.

traditional ruben sandwich

You will need the following ingredients per sandwich:
2 slices rye bread, buttered
lettuce
3 thin slices pastrami
2 slices Swiss cheese
1 tablespoon warmed sauerkraut
parsley to garnish

Place one slice of bread on a serving plate. Top with lettuce, pastrami, Swiss cheese and sauerkraut. Top with the second slice of bread and garnish with finely chopped parsley.

Paella is a traditional Spanish dish made with Calasparra — a plump, short-grain rice. This variation, using orzo instead of rice, came from one of those nights when I had no food in the house except for chicken thighs and prawns in the freezer, and a few odds and ends in the pantry.

prawn and chicken asian orzo paella

Serves 6

sesame oil for frying
4 shallots, finely sliced
1cm piece ginger, finely diced
2 cloves garlic, crushed and diced
2 boneless, skinless chicken thighs, diced
250g orzo
500ml chicken stock
2 teaspoons Spanish smoked paprika
2 cups prepared prawns
1/3 cup chopped coriander
juice of 2 lemons
salt and pepper to taste
light soy sauce and extra coriander to garnish

In a heavy-based frying pan, heat a little sesame oil and sauté the shallots, ginger and garlic. Add the chicken and cook until well browned on all sides. Add the orzo and stir through to coat with oil. Add a little stock and the paprika and stir to combine. Over a medium heat, continue to cook, adding more stock as required.

When the orzo is just about al dente add the prawns, coriander and lemon juice. Season with salt and pepper. Serve immediately topped with light soy sauce and coriander.

This soup is also known as the 'Jewish penicillin' — so traditional, yet so good.

get well chicken soup

Serves 6

1 chicken, cut into pieces
3.5L cold water
4 carrots, peeled and cut into quarters
1 leek, chopped and cleaned
2 onions, peeled and cut into halves
3 parsnips, peeled and cut into quarters
fresh parsley
bay leaves
salt and peppercorns

Put the chicken into a very large saucepan, cover with the water. Bring to the boil, reduce the heat and simmer for 15 minutes, removing any scum that forms. Add all the vegetables, herbs and seasoning. Cover and simmer for 1½ hours. Remove the chicken and allow to cool. Once cooled, remove the flesh from the bones. Discard the bones and skin. Cover the flesh and put into the fridge.

Return the stock to the heat and cook covered for a further 30 minutes. Strain the stock, discarding the vegetables. Chill and refrigerate overnight. A solid top of fat will form. Remove this.

Transfer the stock back to the saucepan. Put in the chicken and heat through. This can either be served with egg noodles or matzo balls.

Note: Matzo ball mix is available in good supermarkets. Make to packet instructions.

The point of this dish is its simplicity. People always ask me why I insist on using the best possible ingredients available. This dish answers that question. It is simple but incredibly flavoursome. Try it and you will understand what I mean.

bruschetta pomodoro

bread
garlic
tomatoes
basil
olive oil
freshly cracked pepper

Slice bread and grill, preferably over flame. Rub raw garlic into the still-warm bread to infuse the flavour.
  Slice the tomatoes and layer over the bread. Lay torn basil leaves on top and drizzle with olive oil and freshly cracked pepper.

I have included this to remind people about traditional methods of preserving foods. Not everything has to come out of a can.

preserved tomatoes

Makes 4 jars

1.5kg Roma tomatoes
6 cloves garlic, lightly crushed
a few basil leaves, fresh oregano
  and bay leaves

Pack the tomatoes into sterilised jars, layering with the garlic and herbs. Remove any air bubbles with a knife blade and seal jars.
  Stand sealed jars upright in a saucepan and cover with cold water. Bring the water to the boil and continue boiling for 30 minutes. Remove from the heat and cool completely before removing jars from the saucepan.
  Check that the lids have sealed correctly and store in a cool dark pantry. They will keep for several months.

This easy pasta bake is something that the whole family will enjoy. Wild Italian oregano is available from speciality food stores and gives this dish a sweet, herbaceous flavour. The word 'oregano' is Greek for 'joy of the mountain'.

cheesy smoked chicken pasta bake

Serves 6

1 onion, diced
olive oil for frying
1 red capsicum, seeds removed, roughly diced
1 teaspoon wild Italian oregano
2 smoked chicken breasts,
  skin removed, sliced
1 cup cottage cheese
2 big handfuls baby spinach
125g mozzarella, shredded
rind of 1 lemon
salt and pepper to taste
250g penne or perroni pasta,
  cooked to packet instructions
1 cup grated Parmesan cheese

Set oven to 175ºC. Lightly grease a large baking dish.

In a heavy-based frying pan, sauté the onion in a little oil until tender. Add capsicum and oregano. Sauté until capsicum softens a little, approximately 3 to 4 minutes. Transfer to a large bowl. Add the smoked chicken breast, cottage cheese, spinach, mozzarella, lemon rind and salt and pepper. Add everything to the pasta and, using a metal spoon, gently fold through until well combined.

Transfer to prepared dish and sprinkle the Parmesan over the top. Cover with foil and bake for 35 minutes. Uncover and cook for a further 8 to 10 minutes until slightly browned.

I love salsas. Salsa is the Mexican word for sauce. I like them because they are a fresh, textured taste sensation and they add another dimension to food, especially grilled foods. They should be diced rather than blended. It is important to use produce that is ripe but not over-ripe to maintain the texture. Salsas are also about contrast of flavour — sweet and sour, mild and hot. Try the pear and avocado salsa on barbecued chicken or even on a Mexican chocolate tart, or the watercress, radish and mandarin salsa on grilled or pan-fried fish. The chestnut, feijoa and mint salsa is exceptional with lamb.

pear and avocado salsa

½ pear, diced
1 avocado (firm but ripe), peeled, stone removed, diced
rind and juice of 1 lime
⅓ cup chopped coriander leaves

Combine everything and gently fold together.

watercress, radish and mandarin salsa

1 cup picked watercress, leaves roughly chopped
1 cup radish, finely diced
4 mandarins, peeled, segmented and chopped

Combine everything and gently fold together.

Fresh chestnuts can either be boiled or roasted. Seeing chestnuts being roasted in cities in Europe is a wonderful, warming, winter experience. There always seems to be someone there roasting chestnuts. However, this recipe is best made with French tinned chestnuts, which are now available in good supermarkets.

chestnut, feijoa and mint salsa

½ cup diced cooked chestnuts
½ cup peeled diced feijoas
2 tablespoons finely chopped mint
juice of ½ lemon

Combine everything and gently fold together.
   Note: If using fresh chestnuts, I would suggest boiling them. Boil for 40 to 45 minutes and allow to cool before peeling and dicing.

This is a hearty winter soup. By blending only half of the soup you can achieve a really nice texture.

chickpea and pumpkin soup

Serves 4

1 cup dried chickpeas
2 large onions, diced
olive oil
1½L water or vegetable stock
1 medium pumpkin, skinned,
  seeds removed, diced
1 teaspoon cumin seeds, crushed
1 teaspoon coriander seeds, crushed
½ teaspoon ground nutmeg
½ cup chopped coriander
salt and pepper to taste

Cover the chickpeas with cold water and leave to stand overnight.
   When you are ready to make the soup, sauté the onion in a little olive oil. Add the water or stock, pumpkin, drained chickpeas and spices. Cover and simmer until the chickpeas are tender, approximately one hour.
   Remove from the heat. Blend half of the mixture in a blender or food processor and return to the pot with the coriander. Stir through. Season with salt and pepper.

This recipe can be made into large cakes to be served as a main course, or smaller cakes to be served as finger food. Either way, they are delicious. The cooking time will vary depending on the size of the cakes. The following instructions are for large cakes.

thai pumpkin and chicken cakes

Makes 6–8 large cakes or 20 small cakes

1 bunch fresh coriander
3 kaffir lime leaves, chopped
1 stalk lemongrass, chopped
salt and pepper to taste
3 tablespoons sweet chilli sauce
3 cups grated pumpkin
100g chicken mince
1 cup breadcrumbs (may not need the whole cup
   depending on the dryness of the pumpkin)
¼ cup canola oil
2 tablespoons sesame oil

Set oven to 200°C.
   In a food processor blend together the coriander, lime leaves, lemongrass, salt, pepper and chilli sauce. Add the pumpkin, chicken mince and breadcrumbs. Shape into cakes. Heat the oils together in a frying pan and brown the cakes on both sides. You will need to do this in batches.
   Place the cakes on a baking tray and bake for 20 minutes or until firm and cooked through.
   Serve with dipping sauces.

This is one of our classics and whenever we make it, it flies out the door. It's a great all-year-round salad and is especially good to have at a barbecue.

zarbo stelle pasta salad

Serves 6–8

½ cup sultanas
¼ cup toasted pine nuts
¼ cup sesame seeds
3 tablespoons poppy seeds
1 red capsicum, seeds removed, finely diced
1 green capsicum, seeds removed, finely diced
½ cup chopped Italian parsley
1½ cups stelle pasta, cooked in boiling, salted water
  7 to 10 minutes, stirring occasionally until al dente

Add sultanas, nuts, seeds, capsicum and parsley to the cooked pasta and toss well.
Add the dressing and combine well.

dressing

3 tablespoons raspberry vinegar
⅓ cup olive oil
½ teaspoon ground cumin
½ teaspoon curry powder
½ teaspoon turmeric

Combine all and stir together well.

This is easy to make and you can use virtually any vegetables. Serve with a crisp, green salad.

vegetable torta

Serves 4

baking spray
2 tablespoons polenta
oil
4 shallots, finely sliced
2 cloves garlic, finely sliced
2 courgettes, sliced
2 small bunches asparagus,
  cut into 1.5cm pieces
2 large handfuls spinach
250g mascarpone
250g cottage cheese
4 eggs
½ cup grated Parmesan cheese
pinch of nutmeg
salt and pepper to taste

Set oven to 160°C. Prepare a 24cm springform tin by spraying with baking spray and lightly dusting with polenta.

In a frying pan, heat a little oil and sauté the shallots and garlic until translucent. Add the courgettes and asparagus (reserve the tips to add later) and sauté until just tender. Add spinach and asparagus tips and cook until spinach has wilted. Remove from the heat and set aside.

Beat the mascarpone until smooth and fold in the cottage cheese, eggs, half of the Parmesan, and the nutmeg. Fold through the cooled vegetables and season with salt and pepper. Pour the mixture into prepared tin and sprinkle over the remaining Parmesan cheese.

Bake for 30 to 35 minutes until golden brown and cooked.

Because of the wetness of the egg/cheese mix this will be quite wobbly when it comes out of the oven. Refrigerate when cool and it will set after a few hours.

Probably the best way to reheat this is to slice into pieces and, dare I say it, microwave one piece at a time on high power for two minutes.

delidelights

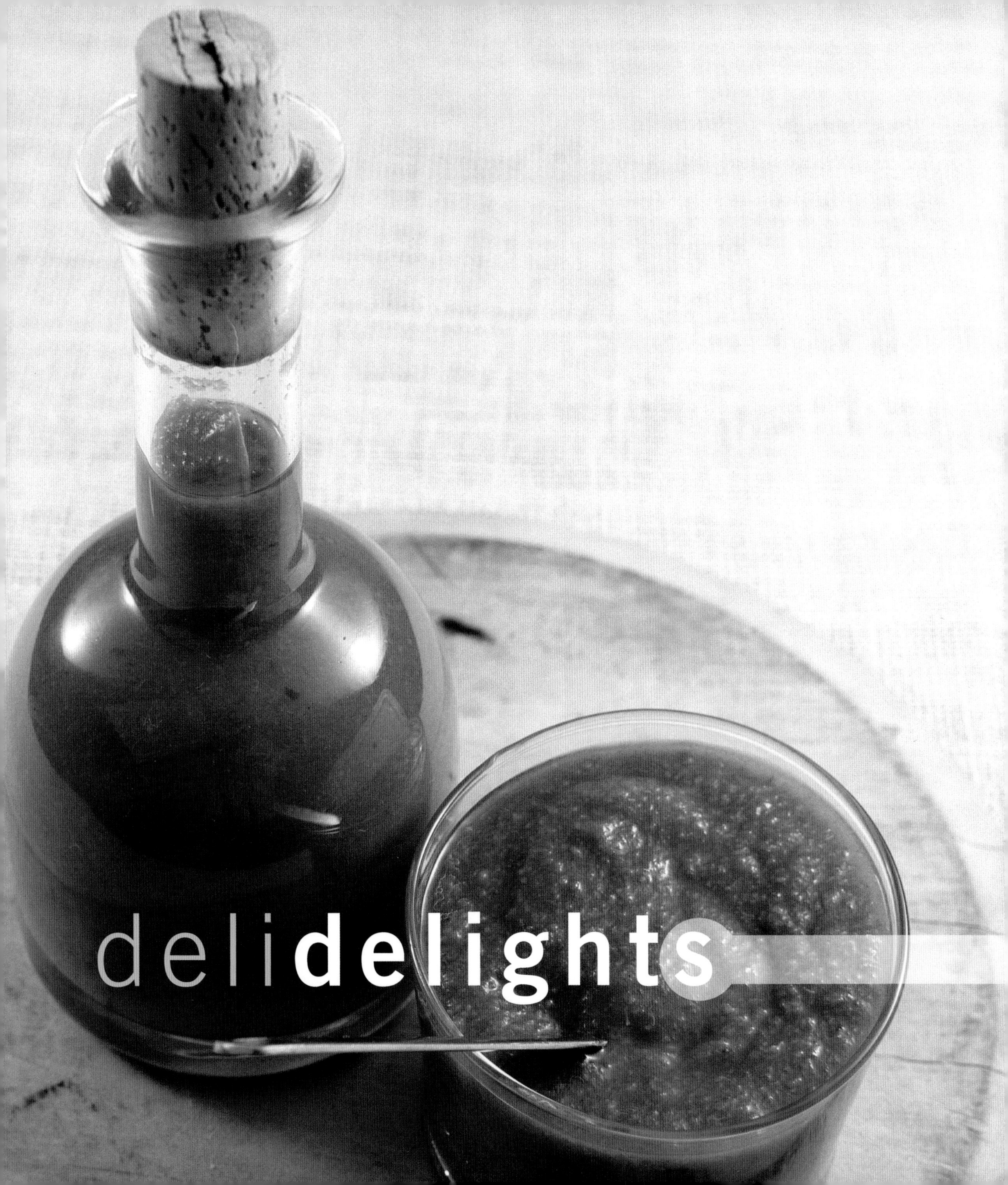

delidelights

Delicatessens and food markets are fascinating places for foodies. I am constantly looking for new products and ideas and adapting what I see, using whatever ingredients are available to me. On a recent trip to London, a friend took me to Borough Market where I purchased some sardines. Back at her house I lightly sautéed the sardines with some green olives, garlic and white wine. You'll find the recipe on page 76, using piper. We also bought some sheep's-milk cheeses which would be a perfect accompaniment for the pumpkin, orange and bay jam on page 64.

There is also a selection of basic dressings. By understanding how to put together a simple dressing and how flavours work together, it is possible for the home cook to create an impressive meal with ease.

New Zealand is now internationally recognised as a world leader in food styles and trends — Kiwis have always had an inventive, creative streak and are well known for their can-do attitude. I encourage you to experiment with these recipes. They are most suitable for entrées, light meals and food platters for entertaining. But remember, if you are putting together a platter of food it is going to be the first thing your guests see — make it interesting, make it visual!

This is a classic Tuscan dish. Be warned: it is very rich. I suggest serving it as an entrée, perhaps with the decadent beef casserole. (See page 114.)

tuscan duck breast with pecorino

Serves 4 as an entrée

2 duck breasts, skin removed
4 slices pancetta
2–3 tablespoons olive oil
4 cloves garlic, crushed
100g pecorino (approximately),
  diced into 1cm cubes
a splash of white wine (more if necessary)
6 sage leaves to garnish

Cut the duck breasts into 6 even-sized strips. Tear the pancetta into bite-sized pieces. In a heavy-based frying pan, heat the olive oil and add the garlic and the pancetta. Gently fry until slightly browned and crispy. Remove from the pan and set aside.

   Add the duck to the pan and brown on all sides. Add the cheese and toss for a few minutes until all is well coated. Pour the wine into the pan and toss together. Continue cooking, adding more wine if necessary, and continue this process until all the wine has evaporated and the duck is cooked. Add the cooked pancetta to the pan. Toss and heat through. Garnish with sage leaves.

Piquillo peppers are available either tinned or bottled from good supermarkets and speciality food stores. You can use small, fresh red capsicums that you blister and peel. Covered in olive oil these will keep refrigerated for several months. However, I prefer to eat them a few hours after making them. It is hard to give exact amounts for this recipe as it varies, depending on the size of the peppers.

spanish piquillo peppers stuffed with tuna

Makes 15–20

250g tinned tuna
1 small tin anchovies
juice and rind of 1 lemon
1 small red chilli, seeds removed,
    finely sliced
2 cloves garlic, finely diced
2 tablespoons capers, chopped
2 tablespoons parsley, chopped
2 tablespoons olive oil
8–12 canned piquillo peppers

Put the tuna into a bowl and mash with the back of a fork.
    Chop the anchovies and add to the bowl. Combine all ingredients together (except peppers) and mix thoroughly. Spoon mixture into piquillo peppers and arrange on a platter.

This is a traditional Swedish way of preserving salmon. However, I have changed it to include some of the flavours that we now commonly use. Serve cold as part of an antipasto platter.

gravlax with coriander root and szechwan pepper

Serves 6–8 with crusty bread as a lunch or many more as part of a platter

3 tablespoons sea salt
1 tablespoon Szechwan pepper
3 tablespoons grated palm sugar
2 coriander roots (with stems), finely chopped
2 tablespoons gin
1kg piece fresh salmon, bones and tail removed, cut into halves

Crush the sea salt and pepper in a mortar and pestle and mix in palm sugar, coriander and gin. Press into the salmon. Layer the spiced salmon sides together and cover with plastic wrap. Weight down and refrigerate. The curing process will take three days and the salmon should be turned twice each day. When ready remove from plastic wrap and scrape off excess salt mix.

Using a very sharp knife on an angle, slice the gravlax as thinly as possible. When the blade of the knife hits the skin straighten the knife so that the salmon slides off leaving the skin. Layer slices between plastic wrap. It will keep for up to one week refrigerated.

This is based on the traditional pissaldière,
a speciality of the Nice region of France.
With a crisp salad, it makes a delicious lunch.

onion and anchovy tart

Serves 6

6 sheets of ready-rolled puff pastry
2 egg yolks, lightly beaten
1 batch caramelised onion
2 tomatoes, finely sliced (12 slices)
anchovy fillets
capers

Set oven to 180°C.

Cut the pastry sheets in half. Take six pieces of
pastry and cut out a window leaving a 1cm-wide
'frame'. Brush the other pieces with egg yolk and neatly
place the pastry frames on top and brush with egg.
Using a fork, pierce the bases several times to prevent
them from rising during cooking.

Bake 6 to 8 minutes until frame has risen and pastry
is browned.

Arrange the caramelised onion, tomatoes, anchovy
fillets and capers on the pastry and serve immediately.

caramelised onion

3 red onions, sliced
2 cloves garlic, sliced
oil for frying
½ teaspoon herbes de Provence
1 teaspoon balsamic vinegar
1 teaspoon brown sugar
1 tablespoon white wine

Sauté the onion and garlic in a little oil until translucent. Add the herbs, balsamic vinegar, brown sugar and wine. Cook
over a medium heat for 25 to 30 minutes until lightly caramelised.

Dips are an ideal addition to a platter served with the pita crisps below.
This is also good as a sandwich spread.

roast pumpkin, smoked paprika and cashew dip

Makes approximately 3 cups

¼ pumpkin, peeled and cubed
2 cloves garlic, crushed
oil to coat pumpkin
salt and pepper to taste
½ teaspoon Spanish smoked paprika
½ teaspoon ground cumin
rind and juice of 1 lemon
2 tablespoons olive oil
⅓ cup toasted cashew nuts (reserve a few for garnish)

Set oven to 160°C. Toss the pumpkin and the garlic in a little oil and season. Bake for 20 to 25 minutes until tender. Toss a few times during cooking to ensure all is cooked evenly. Allow to cool.

   Place the pumpkin into a blender or food processor and pulse. Add the paprika, cumin seeds, lemon rind and juice and second measure of olive oil into the food processor and blend. Add the cashew nuts and blend to desired consistency.

   Transfer to a bowl and garnish with extra cashews. Serve at room temperature.

black olive salsa

Makes approximately 2 cups

1 cup tomatoes, deseeded and diced
½ cup kalamata olives,
   pitted and diced
½ yellow capsicum, seeds and
   membrane removed, diced
juice of ½ lemon
1 tablespoon capers, chopped
1–2 tablespoons olive oil
   (enough to blend)
cracked pepper

Place all ingredients in a bowl and combine well.

oven-baked pita crisps

pita breads, split and each
   circle cut into 12 pieces
¼ cup garlic oil or light olive oil
½ tablespoon paprika
½ tablespoon zahtar
½ tablespoon sumac
salt

Set oven to 160°C.

   Brush both sides of the pieces of pita bread with oil. Divide into three groups. Sprinkle each group with one of the three spices and season with salt. Bake, turning a couple of times until lightly browned on both sides, 12 to 15 minutes. Allow to cool on a wire rack and store in an airtight container.

I used to serve this as an entrée in a restaurant that I worked in many years ago, but Kiwis seem a little apprehensive about polenta. Cooked properly it can be very good. Experiment — try cooking it with white wine in the water, with fresh herbs or crumbled blue cheese.

grilled polenta with slow-roasted tomatoes, gorgonzola and prosciutto

Serves 4

1.5L boiling water
1 teaspoon salt
225g instant polenta
olive oil
8 slow-roasted tomatoes
Gorgonzola, about 1 tablespoon per serve (more to taste)
8 slices prosciutto, grilled

Grease a 15cm-square brownie tin.
   Bring the salted water to the boil. In a steady stream, pour the polenta into the water, whisking to incorporate and making sure no lumps form. Whisk vigorously until the mixture is thick, rich and creamy, approximately 10 minutes. Pour into prepared baking dish and spread evenly. Allow to cool completely. Turn out and trim the edges and cut into four pieces. Brush with olive oil and sear on a grill plate.
   Set oven to 160°C.
   Place the pieces of grilled polenta on a greased baking tray grilled-side up. Place a slow-roasted tomato and some Gorgonzola on top. Bake for 5 to 7 minutes until the cheese begins to melt. Remove from the oven, place on individual serving plates and garnish with the prosciutto.

slow-roasted tomatoes

8 tomatoes, cut into halves
2 cloves garlic, very finely diced
salt and pepper to taste
olive oil to drizzle

Set the oven to 150°C.
   Place the tomatoes cut side up on a baking tray. Drizzle with the olive oil and sprinkle over the salt and pepper and the garlic. Slowly roast for about 50 minutes.

There are many ways to make sushi. Traditionally it is rolled using a bamboo mat. Otherwise a clean, dry tea towel can be used. I first made sushi probably 20 years ago and don't use either. On a clean dry board I place a sheet of nori and a good-sized spoonful of the prepared rice onto the sheet. With slightly dampened hands, I smooth the rice out. Starting at the end nearest me, I work outwards. It is important that the rice is spread evenly over two-thirds of the nori. Next, using the back of a teaspoon handle, I make a small track through the rice at about 2cm from the nearest end. Then I place a little wasabi and the other fillings in the channel. It is important not to put in too much. Carefully, I roll it up as tightly as possible. Then I lightly wet the far end of the nori to seal the roll. You can experiment with shapes, fillings and toppings.

sushi

This recipe will make 25–30 pieces

sushi rice

2 cups sushi rice
2 cups cold water
½ cup rice wine vinegar
2 tablespoons sugar
2 teaspoons salt

Soak the rice in cold water for 10 minutes. Drain and transfer to a heavy-based saucepan. Add water, cover and bring to the boil. Lower the heat and simmer until all the water has been absorbed, approximately 7 minutes.

Meanwhile, combine the vinegar, sugar and salt in a bowl and stir with a fork until the sugar has dissolved.

Transfer the cooked rice to a large ceramic dish. Flatten out with a wooden spatula. Pour over the vinegar mix. Using the spatula, mix through thoroughly for at least 5 minutes. Allow to cool stirring occasionally to prevent the rice from clumping.

For sushi fillings pretty much anything goes. However, I personally don't like avocado in sushi.

fillings

asparagus	prawns	smoked eel
cucumber, sliced	red capsicum, sliced	snow peas, sliced
flaked hot-smoked salmon	salmon caviar	spring onion, sliced
lumpfish roe	sliced salmon	wasabi paste

This is very easy to make, and stored correctly will last for ages. It's also very versatile, used in sandwiches and on a cheeseboard.

pumpkin, orange and bay jam

Makes 4 jars

1.5kg pumpkin, skinned and
   seeds removed
1kg sugar
juice and rind of 1 orange
rind of 2 lemons
12 bay leaves
pinch of freshly grated nutmeg
1 cinnamon stick
$1\frac{1}{5}$ teaspoons cracked pepper

Cook pumpkin, sugar and orange juice over a low heat stirring occasionally for 45 minutes. Blend and return to the saucepan. Add orange and lemon rind and orange juice, bay leaves, nutmeg, cinnamon stick and pepper. Cook a further 25 minutes until thickened. Remove cinnamon stick.

Pack into sterilised jars. Remove any air bubbles with a knife blade and seal jars.

Stand sealed jars upright in a saucepan and cover with cold water. Bring the water to the boil and boil for 20 minutes. Remove from the heat and allow to cool completely before removing jars from the saucepan.

Check that the lids have sealed correctly and store in a cool dark pantry.

Many people think that quince originally came from Europe. In fact, it comes from South-East Asia. It is an unusual fruit — inedible raw, it takes on an entirely different form when cooked, with an amazing taste and colour. Try this on grilled chicken or on cold meats and vegetables.

chinese-spiced quince sauce

Makes 1.5 litres

1.5kg quince
2 cups rice wine vinegar
½ cup light soy sauce
1 spice bag, containing:
   1 teaspoon Szechwan peppercorns,
   1 cinnamon quill,
   6 star anise,
   2 pieces dried galangal
¾ cup sugar
2 cups water

Wash the quince well to remove any fluff. Cut into quarters and remove core. Place quince, vinegar, soy sauce and spice bag in a very large non-reactive saucepan. Bring to the boil and continue boiling for 35 minutes. Remove the spice bag and blend with a hand-held whizz. Return to the heat and add sugar and water. Return to the boil, reduce heat and simmer for 30 minutes. Add extra water to obtain desired consistency.

Cool and pour into sterilised bottles. Seal bottles and store in a cool, dark pantry.

Either you are into chicken livers, or you are not. If you are, try this — it is incredibly rich, but extremely good. It is ideal served as a lunch or brunch dish.

chicken livers with spinach, feta and sun-dried tomatoes

Serves 4

olive oil and butter for frying
500g chicken livers, trimmed and coated with flour
½ cup white wine
150g sun-dried tomatoes
1 tablespoon balsamic vinegar
salt and pepper to taste
4 cups baby spinach
1 tablespoon chopped fresh oregano
½ cup feta, diced

In a frying pan, heat equal amounts of olive oil and butter. Cook the livers in batches, turning regularly to brown all sides. The livers should be crispy on the outside and pink in the middle. Drain the livers on paper towels.

Add the wine to deglaze the pan. When the liquid has reduced by one-third, place the livers back in the pan with the sun-dried tomatoes and balsamic vinegar. Season to taste with salt and pepper. Add the spinach and oregano and toss through.

Serve on grilled bruschetta, pouring over any extra juices.

This is a real blast from the past. Serve as a main with a yummy tomato-based sauce and grilled vegetables, or make small ones to have as part of a tapas platter.

spanish-style beef olives

Serves 4

2 cloves garlic, diced
olive oil
1 cup mushrooms, finely chopped
½ cup green olives, finely chopped
75g breadcrumbs
1 egg, beaten
1½ teaspoons Spanish smoked paprika
½ teaspoon ground cumin
salt and pepper to taste
4 pieces topside steak, or schnitzel
extra oil for frying
½ cup white wine

Set oven to 160°C.

In a frying pan, sauté the garlic in a little oil until tender. Add the mushrooms and sauté until tender. Transfer to a bowl and add the olives, breadcrumbs, egg, paprika, cumin and salt and pepper.

Lay the meat out on a board. If using schnitzel that is full length, cut each piece in half to allow two beef olives per serving. Divide the stuffing mixture into four or eight.

Place stuffing onto the end of each piece of meat. Roll up the meat and secure with cocktail sticks.

In an oven-proof frying pan, heat a little oil and sauté the beef olives until well browned. Remove from the pan and deglaze the pan with the wine.

When the liquid has reduced by half, place the beef olives back in the pan and cover with foil. Bake for 20 minutes until well cooked, turning occasionally.

Pâtés are always popular. The addition of tomato paste and cream cheese make this extremely rich.

tuscan chicken liver pâté

Makes approximately 2 cups

25g butter
1 small onion, diced
2 cloves garlic
300g chicken livers, trimmed and cleaned
2 bay leaves
2 tablespoons capers
4 anchovy fillets
2 tablespoons brandy
2 tablespoons water
1 tablespoon tomato paste
2 tablespoons cream cheese
½ teaspoon chopped rosemary
½ teaspoon chopped sage
salt and pepper

In a heavy-based frying pan, melt the butter and sauté the onion and garlic until translucent. Add the chicken livers and brown on all sides. Add the bay leaves, capers and anchovy fillets and stir regularly until the livers are just cooked.

Deglaze the pan with the brandy and water, if required. Add the tomato paste and heat through. Add the cream cheese and cook until all is combined. You may need to add a little extra water at this stage.

Remove the bay leaves and add the chopped herbs. Transfer to a food processor and lightly pulse. I prefer this blended, but with some texture.

smoked fish pâté

Makes approximately 2 cups

75g softened butter
125g cream cheese
juice and rind of 2 lemons
1½ teaspoons wasabi paste
2 tablespoons chopped coriander
pepper and salt to taste
250g smoked fish, skinned, boned and flaked

This pâté is best made a day before serving — this allows the wasabi flavour to develop.
Serve both these pâtés with pita crisps. (See page 58.)

Blend the butter and cream cheese together until smooth. Add everything except the fish and blend well. Finally, add the fish and pulse until well incorporated.

Dressings are about creating an instant flavour hit! By mastering a few basic techniques you will be able to add a spark to foods that will impress family and friends. I am a bit of a traditionalist in that I believe dressings should stay on salads and in sandwiches. However, in saying this, I am all for salads with lots of interesting things that make a complete meal. The egg-based dressings should be refrigerated and used within a few days, but the oil-based dressings will last stored in a cool dark pantry for a few weeks.

dressings

creamy avocado dressing

1 avocado
1 egg
juice of ½ lemon
¾ cup grapeseed oil
salt and pepper to taste

In a food processor, blend the avocado, egg and lemon juice until smooth. In a constant stream, blend in oil. Season with salt and pepper.

   Alternatively, blend half the avocado with the egg and lemon juice and add the other half with the salt and pepper to thicken the dressing. (See fop left.)

anchovy dressing

8–10 anchovy fillets, depending on taste
1 clove garlic
cracked pepper
1 egg yolk
1 cup olive oil
juice of 1 lemon

Blend the anchovies, garlic and pepper until smooth. Add the egg yolk and blend. In a constant stream, blend in oil. Add lemon juice and blend to desired consistency.

   Note: The creamy avocado and anchovy dressings need to be consistent and pourable. A level of skill is required to achieve this, however, once you've got the hang of it you'll never forget. If these mayonnaise-style dressings are too thick they can be thinned by drizzling in a little hot water. (See bottom left.)

thai sweet chilli sauce

200g sugar
1½ cups rice wine vinegar
3–4 chillies, seeds removed, sliced
4 cloves garlic, sliced

Heat the sugar and the vinegar until boiling.

   Add the chillies and garlic and reduce heat. Simmer for 10 minutes and allow to cool. (See top right.)

tarragon sherry vinaigrette

2 tablespoons chopped fresh tarragon
60ml sherry vinegar
1 clove garlic, chopped
100ml olive oil
salt and pepper

Combine all and mix well. (See top left.)

double-soy vinaigrette

75ml Japanese light soy
50ml Chinese dark soy
100ml Chinese rice wine vinegar
2 cloves garlic, finely chopped

Combine all and mix well. (See bottom left.)

lemon honey vinaigrette

¼ cup lemon juice
¼ cup white wine vinegar
⅓ cup honey
salt and pepper
1–1½ cups grapeseed oil

In a bowl mix the lemon juice, vinegar, honey, salt and pepper.
    Pour in the oil and whisk until well combined. (See top right.)

balsamic, olive oil, garlic and basil dressing

2 cloves garlic, finely chopped
50ml balsamic
100ml olive oil
2 tablespoons chopped basil
salt and pepper

Combine all. (See bottom right.)

Ask your fish shop to gut and fillet the fish. But, if you prefer, it is very simple to do yourself: Cut off the head and tail. Using a sharp knife insert the blade into the fish beside the anal fin and cut fish open up to its head. Next, cut down to the tail. Rinse under a cold tap, removing the gut. Using your thumb, rub along the spine to separate the spine from the flesh. Lay the flattened fillet on a board and using the back of your knife scrape away any remaining bones. Rinse well under cold water and pat dry with paper towels. With a loaf of crusty French bread to soak up any juices, this is ideal as an entrée.

marinated piper

Serves 2

½ cup extra virgin olive oil
1 tablespoon chopped parsley
juice of 2 or 3 lemons
rind of 1 lemon
cracked pepper
4 piper, filleted

Combine the oil, parsley, lemon juice and rind and pepper. Place a little of the oil mixture on the base of a container that will neatly fit two of the fish so that they sit flat and do not overlap. Prepare the fish as above. Place two fillets side by side and pour over more of the oil mix. Place the remaining two fillets on top. Pour over the remaining oil. Refrigerate for at least 24 hours before serving. Serve at room temperature.

pan-fried piper

Serves 2

oil
2 cloves garlic, finely sliced
½ cup green olives
1 small red chilli, seeds removed,
   finely sliced
4 piper, filleted
white wine

In a frying pan large enough to accommodate all four
fish, heat the oil. Otherwise cook in two batches. Add
the garlic, olives and chilli and, over a medium heat,
fry until translucent. Add the fillets and sear on each
side for about one minute. Finish off with a decent
splash of white wine and serve immediately.

It is common in South-East Asian cooking to use the roots of coriander without the tops as they have a very intense flavour. They need to be well cleaned and very finely sliced.

vine leaves with vietnamese beef

Makes 20

oil
2 cloves garlic, finely diced
2 coriander roots, finely chopped
250g beef mince
2 teaspoons Szechwan peppercorns, crushed
1 teaspoon grated ginger
1 teaspoon turmeric
3 tablespoons coriander, chopped
2 tablespoons palm sugar, grated
2 spring onions, finely sliced
½ cup bean sprouts, roughly chopped
20 vine leaves (available in jars from speciality food stores and some supermarkets)

In a heavy-based frying pan, heat a little oil and sauté the garlic and coriander root. Add the beef and stir with a wooden spoon to ensure that the mince is all broken up. Continue until the meat is well cooked and any fat has evaporated. Add the pepper, ginger and turmeric and cook until well combined. Add the coriander, palm sugar, onion and sprouts and cook a further 4 to 5 minutes until all is well combined.

Rinse the vine leaves well and stand in cold water for 30 minutes to remove excess brine. Drain well and pat dry with paper towel.

Spoon a generous tablespoon of the beef mixture into each leaf and roll up.

Serve with a suitable dipping sauce.

This is a classic deli-style salad and is best served with a loaf of crusty French bread or ciabatta.

shredded chicken and pesto salad

Serves 4

2 large chicken breasts, skin removed
2 cloves garlic, finely chopped
1 ball mozzarella, hand shredded
4 tablespoons pesto
1 pickled lemon, rinsed and very finely sliced
salt and pepper

Poach the chicken breasts in seasoned water until cooked and allow to cool completely. When cool, very finely hand shred.

Combine in a large bowl with all the other ingredients.

Quinoa is a great grain and I particularly like it in this tabbouleh.

tabbouleh with quinoa, mint and pomegranate dressing

Serves 6

250g quinoa
1 cup chopped parsley
⅔ cup chopped mint
1 large cucumber, seeds removed, diced
4 large tomatoes, seeds removed, diced

Cook quinoa in boiling, salted water for approximately 7 minutes. Drain well and set aside to cool. When cool combine with all ingredients. Toss dressing through salad.

pomegranate dressing

⅓ cup pomegranate concentrate
⅓ cup white wine
1 clove garlic, very finely chopped
salt and pepper to taste

Combine all ingredients and mix well.

Serve this as an entrée to impress your family and friends.

grilled asparagus with grana padano, quails' eggs and blue-cheese dressing

Serves 6

3 bunches asparagus, ends trimmed
olive oil to coat asparagus
½ cup shaved Grana Padano
12 quail eggs, hard boiled, peeled and halved
salt and pepper to taste
baby spinach

Toss the asparagus in the oil and season with salt and pepper. Cook on a grill plate and set aside to cool.
   Assemble as individual servings with dressing on the side.

blue-cheese dressing

1 egg yolk
⅔ cup oil
⅓ cup creamy blue cheese, crumbled
salt and pepper to taste

Whisk the egg yolk in a bowl. In a constant stream, whisk in the oil to form a smooth mayonnaise. Fold through the blue cheese and season with salt and pepper.

Zarbo
DELICATESSEN • CAFE

Zarbo
DELICATESSEN • CAFE

Zarbo
DELICATESSEN • CAFE

Zarbo
DELICATESSEN • CAFE

fruit
$1.00 Bag
2.00 Bag

Pineapples
$ 2.00 each

PINEAPPLES
Dole
PINEAPPLES

allthingsgreen

allthingsgreen

Salads are a huge part of what we do at Zarbo. In the previous two chapters I've included some classic Zarbo salads. Here are some more substantial salads that aren't just a summer thing — they can be enjoyed all year round as simple, satisfying meals or side dishes. For example, the roasted pumpkin with chermoulla can be served hot or cold.

The exciting array of produce now available means that we can really expand what we do. For example, I love the simple, refreshing Asian flavours — lime juice, mint, coriander, chilli and Asian vinegars and sauces.

When thinking of salad ideas think of how flavours will work together and think of texture. I believe that the best salads are simple — not too many ingredients, but with contrasts of flavour and texture. The most important thing to do is use the freshest available produce, and treat it kindly. Remember, leafy green salads should be dressed at the table, but heartier salads need to be prepared a few hours in advance for their flavour to develop.

The contrasting textures of the two rices are what make this salad special.
The broad beans and mint add a delicious sweetness.

rice salad with broad beans and mint

Serves 6

½ cup wild rice, cooked to packet instructions
½ cup basmati rice, cooked to packet instructions
2 cups broad beans, blanched and shelled
½ cup mint leaves, torn

Combine the two cooked rices, beans and mint. Add the dressing and combine well.

dressing

1 large slice of white bread, crusts removed
¼ cup sherry vinegar
2 cloves garlic, crushed
½ cup olive oil
4–6 anchovy fillets, diced (optional)
¼ cup chopped Italian parsley
salt and pepper to taste

Soak the bread in the vinegar for a few minutes. Squeeze the bread dry reserving the vinegar. Place the bread and garlic in a food processor and blend. Pour in the vinegar. Slowly add the oil and pulse regularly. Add the anchovies and parsley and season with salt and pepper. Blend to combine.

Roasted red onions caramelised with balsamic vinegar are fabulous and the feta adds a tartness to the salad. You can make this salad as large or small as you like by varying the quantities.

balsamic red onion salad with feta

Serves 6

4–6 medium-sized red onions, peeled and cut into quarters
balsamic vinegar
brown sugar
salt and pepper to taste
lettuce mix
feta cheese, crumbled
olive oil for drizzling

Place the cut onions into a baking dish, sprinkle with a dash of balsamic vinegar, a little brown sugar and season with salt and pepper. Bake covered at 150ºC for 45 minutes. Remove cover and bake for a further 15 minutes.
   Allow to cool. Toss with salad greens and crumbled feta. Before serving, drizzle with a little olive oil.

When I make this salad I peel the capsicums as well as possible but I try to avoid rinsing them. This helps retain the smoky flavour. The salsa is also great on grilled fish and chicken.

mexican chickpea salad with flamed capsicums and coriander and lime salsa

Serves 6

250g chickpeas
6 capsicums (a mix of colours), seeds removed, cut into quarters

Wash chickpeas and soak overnight. Drain. Cover with cold water and cook in boiling water until tender, approximately 25 minutes then drain.

Chargrill capsicums, peel and tear into pieces. Mix the chickpeas with the capsicum. Toss the coriander and lime salsa through the capsicum and chickpeas.

coriander and lime salsa

3 large tomatoes, seeds removed, finely diced
⅓ cup coriander leaves, chopped
1 large red chilli, seeds removed, finely chopped
rind of 1 lime
juice of 2 limes
salt and pepper to taste

Combine the salsa ingredients and stir well.

I love the rich flavour of roasted pumpkin and, combined with spicy chermoulla, this is a real winner.

roasted pumpkin and red onion salad with chermoulla

Serves 6–8

1 whole pumpkin, peeled, seeded and chopped
grapeseed oil to coat pumpkin
salt and pepper to taste
1 large red onion, peeled and cut into rings

Set oven to 175ºC.
   Toss the pumpkin in a little grapeseed oil and season liberally with salt and pepper. Roast pumpkin until tender and browned, approximately 25 minutes. Toss a few times during cooking.
   Allow the pumpkin to cool a little, then toss through the red onion and the chermoulla.

chermoulla

1 cup parsley
2 cups coriander leaves
2 cloves garlic, bashed and peeled
1½ teaspoons ground turmeric
1 teaspoon ground cumin
juice and rind of 1 lemon
1–1½ cups grapeseed oil

In a food processor, blend the parsley, coriander, garlic, turmeric and cumin. Add the lemon juice and rind, and slowly pour in the grapeseed oil to desired consistency.
   Chermoulla should be smooth and runny, but not too runny. It needs to coat and hold onto the pumpkin.

The colour and texture, combined with the freshness of the dressing, make this salad an interesting addition to a summer lunch.

daikon and melon salad with wasabi and vietnamese mint dressing

Serves 4–6

200g daikon, peeled and sliced as thinly as
  possible
¼ rock melon, peeled and thinly sliced
¼ honeydew melon, peeled and thinly
  sliced
Vietnamese mint, chopped
1 red chilli, seeds removed, finely sliced
  (optional)
whole Vietnamese mint leaves to garnish

Assemble on a platter and garnish with whole
Vietnamese mint leaves and chilli.

wasabi and vietnamese mint dressing

2 tablespoons wasabi paste
juice of lime
8 Vietnamese mint leaves, chopped
2 tablespoons palm sugar, grated
3 tablespoons Chinese rice wine vinegar

Combine all ingredients and stir until the sugar has dissolved.

Rice noodles are so easy to prepare. A simplified version of this salad is ideal for the kids.

Otherwise this can be made into a special meal by adding slices of the blackened Thai

roast duck. (See page 133.)

rice noodle and vegetable salad with sweet and sour dressing

Serves 6

250g rice noodles
½ cup mint leaves
½ cup coriander leaves
1 carrot, julienned
2 stalks celery, julienned
2 red capsicums, seeds removed,
   julienned
1 large handful green beans,
   julienned
1 cup mung bean sprouts
2 tablespoons toasted sesame seeds

Put the noodles in a large bowl, cover with boiling water and allow to stand until cooked. Timing depends upon the size and thickness of the noodles, usually 4 to 7 minutes. Stir occasionally. Once cooked, drain very well and set aside.

Roughly chop the mint and coriander and combine with the prepared vegetables and cooked noodles. Toss the sweet and sour dressing through the salad and sprinkle the sesame seeds over. Serve immediately.

Make this dressing a couple of hours in advance to allow the flavour to develop.

sweet and sour dressing

100ml rice wine vinegar
100g caster sugar
1 small green chilli,
   seeds removed, finely sliced
juice and rind of 1 lemon

Combine all the dressing ingredients and stir until the sugar has dissolved.

The rocket mayo gives this salad a nice, peppery bite.

mixed green salad with rocket mayo

Serves 6

4 large handfuls green beans, trimmed
1 bunch snow peas, trimmed
2 cups broad beans, shelled
16 baby beetroot, trimmed and cleaned
6 baby fennel, tips removed
100g feta, crumbled

Blanch all of the vegetables in boiling, salted water. Refresh in iced water and drain well. Arrange on a platter
with the feta sprinkled through. Toss the rocket mayo through the vegetables.

rocket mayo

2 egg yolks
1 clove garlic, finely diced
1 cup oil
juice and rind of 1 lemon
salt and pepper to taste
2 large handfuls rocket
a little white wine, if required

Blend egg yolks and garlic together. Slowly drizzle in the oil, whisking constantly until mixture thickens.
Add lemon juice and rind and season with salt and pepper. Blend in the rocket.
   If the mixture becomes too thick, blend in a couple of tablespoons of white wine.

This salad is full of fresh flavours. I think it goes particularly well as a side dish with a tagine.

watercress, fennel, orange and red onion salad

Serves 4

6 baby fennel or 1 large fennel bulb, finely sliced
olive oil
4 large oranges, peeled and segmented
2 heads of watercress, cut from their roots but left on their stalks
1 medium red onion, finely sliced

Sauté the fennel in a little hot oil. Remove from the pan and drain on paper towels.
   Combine the cooled fennel, orange, watercress and red onion. Toss dressing through the salad.

dressing

75ml olive oil
juice of ½ orange
75ml sherry vinegar
pinch of sugar
½ teaspoon cracked pepper

Combine all the ingredients.

try**this**at**home**

DELICATESSEN • CAFE

Zarbo

Zarbo
Exotic · Delicious · New Zealand
POPPYSEEDS

trythisathome

Most, but not all, of these recipes require a little bit more effort, but you will be well rewarded.

Most are great to make as casual dinners or suppers for family or friends. The simple penne alla

arrabbiata is easy but so flavoursome and the leek, lemon and caper risotto with pan-fried blue

cod is equally impressive. You will notice that I have used grapeseed oil in a number of recipes

— not only is it cost effective, but it is also very good for you.

The Thai blackened duck is ideal to serve with steamed rice and wok-fried vegetables but, thinly

sliced, the meat can also be used in salads and Asian-style soups. A number of these dishes can

easily be adapted for vegetarians. For example, the Thai lemongrass chicken curry is delicious

when the chicken is substituted with vegetables.

The totally decadent beef casserole is not something you would eat every day but is a great

special-occasion dish. I talk a lot about healthy eating, however, the goose-fat roasted potatoes

are anything but. If you are good most of the time it's all right to occasionally indulge.

Arrabbiata is perhaps the most common of all pasta sauces — and the simplest. Cushla is an expert on this. She always orders it when we are in Italy.

penne alla arrabbiata

Serves 4

olive oil for frying
3 cloves garlic, finely diced
4 shallots, finely sliced
1 small chilli, deseeded and finely sliced
2 400g tins whole peeled tomatoes, hand crushed
salt and pepper to taste
2 tablespoon finely chopped Italian parsley
2 tablespoon finely chopped basil
250g penne, cooked to packet instructions
2 tablespoons shaved Parmesan

In a pan, heat oil and add garlic, shallots and chilli. Cook over a gentle heat until translucent. Add the tomatoes. Season and cook over a medium heat until the sauce has thickened. Add parsley and basil.

Fold through hot pasta. Drizzle with a little extra virgin olive oil and sprinkle shaved Parmesan over.

Seared tuna has become a staple of my diet — I love the simplicity of food like this.
The salad is fresh and cooling, which is great because the nahm jam is extremely hot.

seared tuna with thai salad and nahm jam

Serves 4

tuna, single piece (approximately 500g)
oil
cracked pepper

Rub tuna with a little oil and season with cracked pepper. On a grill plate, sear tuna for two minutes on each side. Set aside to cool, then finely slice.
   Arrange salad ingredients into four bowls. Divide tuna evenly and place on salad. Serve with nahm jam.

thai salad

1 cucumber, ends removed, peeled
1 red capsicum, seeds removed, finely sliced
1 green capsicum, seeds removed, finely sliced
⅓ cup mint leaves
⅓ cup coriander leaves
½ cup mung bean sprouts

Combine all ingredients.

nahm jam

3 red chillies, seeds removed
2 bird's-eye chillies, seeds removed
4 cloves garlic
4 coriander roots, cleaned
3 tablespoons grated palm sugar
3 tablespoons fish sauce
juice of 8 limes

Grind the chillies, garlic and coriander root in a mortar and pestle. Add the sugar and fish sauce and grind until all is well combined. Transfer to a bowl and stir in the lime juice. Transfer to a glass bottle. This will keep for several weeks in the refrigerator.

This is great hot as a main with garlic mash, or sliced cold for a picnic.

chicken breast stuffed with basil, semi-dried tomatoes, goat cheese and prosciutto

Serves 4

4 chicken breasts, skinned and flattened
basil leaves
semi-dried tomatoes
goat cheese
strips of thinly cut prosciutto
Note: The amount of cheese, tomatoes, basil and
  prosciutto will depend on the size of the breasts.

Set the oven to 180°C. Lightly oil a baking dish.

   Flatten the breasts by placing skin side down on a board and, using a sharp knife, cut through the main body of each breast and fold out. Be careful not to cut right through. Do the same at the fillet end of each breast. Place a sheet of foil over the breast and lightly beat with a rolling pin.

   At the fillet end place a line of basil leaves topped with tomatoes and cheese. Squeeze into a tight line. Roll the chicken around the filling as tightly as possible.

   Lay strips of prosciutto on a board and place the chicken roll on the edge. Roll the chicken so that it is wrapped by the prosciutto. Depending upon the size of the chicken breast, you may need to use a second strip of prosciutto.

   Bake for 20 to 25 minutes until the prosciutto is browned and crispy.

This is best made a day in advance, allowed to cool completely and reheated adding a splash more wine. The sauce should be thick, dark and velvety.

totally decadent beef and porcini casserole with goose-fat roasted potatoes

Serves 4

4 tablespoons flour
salt and pepper to taste
4 tablespoons extra virgin olive oil
750g lean beef, diced
175g pancetta, 0.5cm thick slices, diced
1 head garlic, peeled and bashed
16 baby onions or shallots
750ml red wine
500ml beef stock
30g porcini, soak in warm water for
    30 minutes and drained
100ml liquid reserved when draining porcini

Combine the flour with the salt and pepper. Lightly dust the beef with the flour. In a heavy-based saucepan, heat the oil and fry the beef in small batches until well browned on all sides. Remove the beef and set aside, add the pancetta to the pan and brown. Remove and set aside. Add the garlic and onions/shallots and stir until well coated and starting to brown. Remove and set aside.

Add 500ml of the wine and deglaze the pan. Over a high heat, simmer to reduce by one-half. Add the beef stock and the porcini stock and reduce by one-third.

Add the beef to the saucepan, bring to the boil, cover and reduce the heat. Simmer for one hour, checking regularly to make sure there is enough liquid remaining. (It may be necessary to add more wine or stock at this stage.) Add the pancetta, porcini, onions and garlic, more stock if required, and cook a further 20 minutes. Season to taste.

The potatoes absorb a lot of the goose fat, but the flavour justifies the decadence — just not every day!

goose-fat roasted potatoes

4 large potatoes, peeled, cut into halves
1 cup goose fat
1 head garlic, peeled and bashed
½ cup kalamata olives
salt and pepper to taste
1 sprig rosemary, pulled from stalk

Set oven to 150ºC.

Wash potatoes under cold water and dry with paper towels. Score the rounded sides.

In an oven-proof frying pan large enough to take all the potatoes, heat the goose fat. Add the garlic and olives and heat gently. Add the potatoes cut side down, cook for a few minutes. Season with salt and pepper and add the rosemary. Transfer to the oven and bake, basting regularly with the fat until tender and slightly browned.

You can substitute seafood, lamb or vegetables in this curry. This is simple to make and, served with steamed rice, is great on a cold winter's night.

thai lemongrass curry

Serves 4

oil for frying
1 batch simple curry paste
4 chicken breasts, skinned and sliced
2–3 lemongrass stalks, each cut into 3 pieces
2 tablespoons fish sauce
½ cup water
½ cup coconut cream
2 tablespoons grated palm sugar

In a heavy-based saucepan, heat a little oil and sauté the curry paste over a medium heat, stirring regularly for 8 to 10 minutes. If it starts to stick reduce the heat and add a little water. Add the chicken to the saucepan and stir until well combined, approximately 4 to 5 minutes.

Add the lemongrass, fish sauce, water, coconut cream and palm sugar. Stir well. Cook for 35 to 40 minutes until the sauce has thickened and the chicken is cooked. Add more water if necessary.

Serve with Asian greens, steamed rice and garnish with coriander leaves.

This curry paste is very easy to make. I have added a small amount of commercial curry paste to this. It's like adding stock to a casserole – it intensifies the flavour and improves the texture.

simple curry paste

1 onion, diced
1 lemongrass stalk, very finely chopped
2cm piece galangal, finely chopped
4 cloves garlic
1 chilli, or to taste
2 coriander roots, cleaned and finely chopped
2 tablespoons curry paste

Place all ingredients in a food processor and blend as fine as possible.

Risottos are always popular. I particularly like the citrus flavours in this and I love biting into the crunchy capers.

leek, lemon and caper risotto with pan-fried blue cod

Serves 6

olive oil
4 shallots, finely sliced
2 cloves garlic, diced
2 cups arborio rice
1 cup dry white wine
500ml vegetable stock (approximately)
1 leek, white end only cut into 1cm rings
2 tablespoons capers
rind and juice of 2 lemons
knob of butter
⅓ cup Parmesan cheese
salt and pepper to taste

In a heavy-based frying pan, heat a little olive oil and sauté the shallots and garlic until translucent. Add the rice and stir to coat well. Add the wine and stir well to deglaze the pan. Add one cup of stock and the leeks, capers and lemon rind. Keep adding the stock and stirring until all the liquid has been absorbed and the rice is al dente. At this point add the lemon juice, the butter and Parmesan cheese and fold through. Season with salt and pepper.

Arrange pieces of pan-fried blue cod on top and serve immediately.

Serve with wok-fried greens and steamed rice, garnished with crispy fried shallots for a taste treat.

chinese sesame-fried lamb

Serves 4

½ tablespoon Szechwan peppercorns
½ tablespoon star anise
6 cloves garlic, crushed
1½ tablespoons fish sauce
1½ tablespoons soy sauce
2 tablespoons sesame oil
1½ tablespoons grated palm sugar
750g lean lamb, sliced
sesame oil
grapeseed oil

Crush the peppercorns and star anise in a mortar and pestle. Add the garlic, fish and soy sauces, sesame oil and palm sugar. Mix together then add the lamb and coat the lamb with the marinade. Cover and refrigerate over night.

In a wok, heat a little sesame and grapeseed oil. Add lamb and cook in batches. Keep warm.

crispy fried shallots

125ml peanut oil
6–8 large shallots, thinly sliced

In a wok, heat the oil and cook the shallots in small batches until browned and crisp. Drain on absorbent paper towels. Stored in an airtight container, they will keep for 4 to 5 days and can be refreshed in a warm oven.

It's incredible to think how far food has come in New Zealand during the last generation. When I was a kid a ham steak was about as good as it got in the average restaurant. This is a variation on that theme. The tamarind and pineapple chutney has developed from an idea I picked up while holidaying in Fiji a couple of years ago.

grilled ham steaks with tamarind and pineapple chutney

Serves 4

4 ham steaks
baby spinach
slices of fresh pineapple
slow-roasted tomatoes (see page 61)

Heat a grill plate until smoking. Lightly oil the ham steaks and place on the grill. Cook a couple of minutes on each side. Garnish with the baby spinach, pineapple and slow-roasted tomatoes.

Serve with tamarind and pineapple chutney on the side.

tamarind and pineapple chutney

Makes 3 to 4 cups

200g tamarind
1½ cups boiling water
200g dried apples
250g dates
50g ginger
6 cloves garlic
1L red wine vinegar
2 chillies
salt and pepper to taste
½ fresh pineapple, peeled and finely diced

Soak the tamarind in the boiling water for 45 minutes. It is necessary to mash it up once it has started to soften. Strain through a sieve and retain the tamarind juice.

Roughly chop the apples and the dates. Place with the ginger, garlic, vinegar, chillies and salt and pepper in a large, non-reactive saucepan. Bring to the boil, reduce heat and simmer for 30 minutes. Add the pineapple and simmer for a further 20 minutes.

Stored in sterilised jars, this will last up to 18 months.

This is a traditional Indonesian one-pot dish, but I prefer to serve it on a platter with the peanut sauce in the middle.

gado-gado

Serves 6–8 as a platter of finger food

1 pack tofu, drained and patted dry
  with a paper towel
2 tablespoons cornflour
oil for frying
1 cucumber, ends and seeds removed, cut into sticks
1 red capsicum, seeds removed, sliced
1 orange capsicum, seeds removed, sliced
1 bunch asparagus, blanched in boiling water and refreshed in iced water
2 bunches broccolini, blanched in boiling water and refreshed in iced water
1 bunch of spring onions, white ends only,
  blanched in boiling water and refreshed in iced water
1 bunch snake beans, blanched in boiling water and
  refreshed in iced water
4 hard-boiled eggs, cut into quarters
2 Japanese eggplant, finely sliced, brushed with oil and grilled on a grillplate
1 handful okra, brushed with oil and grilled on a grillplate

Dust tofu with cornflour. In a heavy-based frying pan, heat a little oil and brown tofu on all sides. Allow to cool and slice. Arrange everything on a platter around a dish of peanut sauce.

peanut sauce

200g toasted peanuts
1 tablespoon grated ginger
1 small onion, diced
2 red chillies, seeds removed, diced
4 cloves garlic, finely chopped
sesame oil for frying
2 tablespoons fish sauce
2 tablespoons sugar
300ml coconut cream
rind and juice of 1 lemon

Put the toasted peanuts into a food processor and blend until smooth. In a wok, sauté the ginger, onion, chillies and garlic in a little sesame oil until translucent. Add the peanuts and toss to combine. Add the fish sauce and sugar, stirring until well combined. Pour in the coconut cream and lemon rind and juice and continue to stir until thickened.

Cooking leeks slowly not only softens them, it intensifies their flavour. There is just enough sour cream in this to combine all the ingredients without dominating the flavour. Filej is a regional pasta from Calabria in southern Italy.

filej with hot-smoked salmon, leeks and baby spinach

Serves 4

2 tablespoons olive oil
1 clove garlic, finely sliced
2 leeks, cleaned and trimmed into 1cm rings
⅔ cup white wine (extra wine, if required)
1–2 cups baby spinach
2 tablespoons light sour cream
salt and pepper to taste
250g filej pasta, cooked to packet instructions
200g piece of hot-smoked salmon, flaked

In a heavy-based pan, heat the olive oil and add garlic. Fry gently until translucent. Add the leeks, turning after a couple of minutes until lightly browned. Add the wine and simmer until the wine has reduced by half and the leeks are tender. Add the spinach and combine. Stir in the sour cream and season with salt and pepper. Toss through the pasta with the flaked salmon.

You can adapt this simple stir fry using your favourite seasonal vegetables.

wok-fried asian greens with fish

Serves 4

150ml grapeseed oil
50ml sesame seed oil
2 medium fillets blue cod, cut into
    3cm pieces
2 tablespoons sesame oil
4 cloves garlic, finely sliced
1 bird's eye chilli, seeds removed,
    finely sliced
1 red capsicum, seeds removed,
    finely sliced
1 cup snow peas
100ml light soy sauce
50ml fish sauce
50ml Chinese sweetened vinegar
3 heads of bok choy or other
    Asian greens, ends removed,
    cut into quarters
juice of 2 lemons

In a wok, heat first two measures of oil. When it starts to smoke, cook the blue cod in batches for one to two minutes on each side. Remove and drain on absorbent paper. Clean the wok.

Heat the second measure of sesame oil and sauté the garlic and chilli. Add the remaining ingredients and cook quickly over a high heat. Add the reserved fish and heat through.

Serve on steamed rice.

Pickled lemon gives a dish like this a really special citrus flavour.

moroccan meatballs with pumpkin and pickled lemon sauce

Serves 4

meatballs

500g lean beef mince
1 small onion, finely diced
2 cloves garlic, finely diced
½ cup breadcrumbs
1 egg, lightly beaten
½ a pickled lemon, rinsed and finely chopped
  (vary according to taste)
125g feta cheese, crumbled
salt and pepper to taste
olive oil for frying

Combine all the ingredients and form into balls about 1.5cm in diameter.

Heat the olive oil in a heavy-based frying pan and brown the meatballs on all sides until cooked through. You will need to do this in several batches. Drain the meatballs on paper towels.

Serve on steamed rice with pumpkin and pickled lemon sauce.

pumpkin and pickled lemon sauce

1 onion, diced
olive oil
4 cups diced pumpkin, skin and seeds removed,
  cooked and mashed
1 pickled lemon, rinsed and chopped
2 bay leaves
1–1½ cups chicken stock or water
salt and pepper to taste

In a heavy-based frying pan, sauté the onion in a little olive oil until translucent. Add the pumpkin, pickled lemon and bay leaves and one cup of the stock or water. Bring to a simmer adding more water or stock until desired consistency is achieved.

Ducks are now readily available from supermarkets. This recipe uses powdered galangal, which is a mild-flavoured member of the ginger family. You should find it in Asian food stores. Ginger can be substituted.

blackened thai roast duck

Serves 4–6

1 whole duck (approximately 2kg)
1 or 2 oranges
1½ teaspoons Szechwan peppercorns
2 cloves garlic
1 teaspoon sea salt
2 teaspoons powdered galangal
rind and juice of 1 orange
1 tablespoon sesame oil
3 tablespoons light soy sauce
1 tablespoon rice wine vinegar

Set the oven to 180°C.

To prepare the duck, remove the head and lower parts of the wings. Using a fork prick the duck all over. Be careful not to pierce the meat — pierce the skin and fat only. This helps excess fat escape during cooking. Fill the duck's cavity with 1 or 2 oranges cut into halves.

Combine all other ingredients in a mortar and pestle and grind until well combined. Rub this mix into the duck's skin.

Roast duck for 1½ to 2 hours until juices run clear. Baste several times during cooking. Drain off excess fat before serving with steamed rice and stir-fried vegetables.

This is easy to prepare and sensational to eat. With the bones removed the pork loin cooks reasonably quickly. This was cooked on fan bake and I was a bit surprised by the timing, but I have a new oven that seems to be extremely efficient. For well-done I suggest cooking for a further 10 to 15 minutes.

pork loin roasted with fennel, red onion and garlic

Serves 8–10

1 whole pork loin, boned
75ml balsamic vinegar
50ml extra virgin olive oil
1 tablespoon rosemary, chopped
1 tablespoon sage, chopped
½ teaspoon fresh thyme
salt and pepper to taste
2 medium fennel bulbs, roughly chopped
2 large red onions, peeled and sliced into 1cm rings
peel of 1 lemon
6 bay leaves
a few sage leaves
extra oil
sea salt

Set oven to 220ºC.

Using a sharp knife, score the rind of the pork at 1cm intervals. Be careful to only cut through the rind and try not to score the meat.

Mix together the vinegar, oil and herbs. Flip the loin over and generously rub in the vinegar mix and season with salt and pepper.

Place the vegetables in a roasting dish slightly larger than the size of the loin. Place the lemon peel, bay leaves and sage leaves on top of the vegetables and gently place the loin on top of the vegetables skin-side up. Lightly cover the scored skin with the extra olive oil and sprinkle generously with sea salt.

Cook pork for 25 minutes. Reduce heat to 175ºC and cook a further 20 to 25 minutes or until cooked. When the pork has cooked to your desired level remove the loin from the oven and set aside to rest for 10 to 15 minutes before carving.

Return the vegetables to the oven to cook a few minutes longer, until browned.

Hot smoking is easy to do at home. I use a fish smoker that I purchased years ago from a fishing store. It's fun to experiment — play around and work with flavours that you like. Ladies, a smoker is a great Christmas present for your man.

smoked foods

mussels

There are two ways that I like to smoke mussels. First, place cleaned mussels straight into the smoker for 15 to 20 minutes until open and cooked.

Or, steam the mussels until cooked and discard half of the shell. Marinate mussels in half shells in ¼ cup white wine and one tablespoon brown sugar for at least one hour before smoking for 4 to 5 minutes.

chicken thighs

3 tablespoons Worcestershire
  sauce
2 tablespoons brown sugar
4 chicken thighs, skin removed

Combine Worcestershire sauce and sugar and baste the chicken. Refrigerate for at least one hour.

Bring back up to room temperature before smoking for 12 to 15 minutes.

Try this in a sandwich with mango and cos lettuce.

salmon

1 teaspoon salt
4 tablespoons brown sugar
2 tablespoons whisky
1 tablespoon olive oil
freshly cracked pepper
1 side fresh salmon, de-boned

Combine salt, sugar, whisky, oil and
pepper. Rub into salmon and
smoke 8 to 12 minutes, depending
on the size of the salmon.

mushrooms

3 cloves garlic, finely chopped
¾ cup dry white wine
2 tablespoons brown sugar
1 teaspoon dried oregano
6 large Portobello mushrooms

Combine garlic, white wine, sugar
and oregano. Pour over the
mushrooms and marinate for at
least one hour before smoking
for 12 to 15 minutes.

Lamb racks are so easy to prepare, but look dramatic. I have used a citrus theme in this dish by combining sumac and lemon in the rub and lime in the kumara mash. These citrus flavours are balanced by the sweetness of the kumara.

lamb rack with kumara, ginger and lime mash

Serves 4

3 cloves garlic, crushed
rind of 1 lemon, very finely grated
olive oil
2 tablespoons sumac
salt and pepper to taste
4 five-boned French lamb racks

Place the garlic and lemon rind in a mortar and pestle and grind. Add the oil, sumac and seasoning and combine. Rub into the lamb and leave to stand for at least one hour.

Set the oven to 180ºC.

In an oven-proof pan, heat a little olive oil and sear the racks on all sides. Transfer to the oven and cook for 6 to 8 minutes. Remove and lightly cover with tinfoil for 5 minutes before serving.

kumara, ginger and lime mash

1.5kg kumara, peeled and cubed
1cm piece of ginger, peeled and diced
rind and juice of 1 lime
salt and pepper
olive oil

Cook the kumara, ginger and lime rind in boiling, salted water until soft. Remove from the heat and mash. Add lime juice, salt, pepper and olive oil and continue mashing until smooth.

lastthing

last**thing**

In recent years there has been a huge swing towards dark chocolate. Good European cooking

chocolate is now readily available from speciality food stores and is essential in baking — it really

makes a difference to flavour. Included in this chapter are some simple café-style sweet treats, such

as the mini almond crescents and chocolate pretzels. When baking it is important to carefully follow

measurements and cooking times. However, in saying this, no two ovens are the same so I suggest

that you be vigilant.

The rosé and raspberry jelly — another way in which to achieve your daily intake of alcohol — uses

gelatine sheets. These are much easier to use than powdered gelatine and make a much clearer jelly.

Summer fruits aren't as I remember them from my childhood — they just don't seem to be as good.

While they look better, it seems to me that they have lost a lot of their flavour and are not as juicy.

However, it is amazing how adding heat to some fruits brings out their flavour. This is particularly true

of the baked pears for an autumn treat. I have also included a traditional flourless, egg-white based

chocolate torte because it is such a classic. Topped with a mix of yoghurt and date syrup it will make

most occasions special all year round.

This takes a bit of skill and you may need to attempt it a couple of times before getting it right, but it is worth persevering. You have to be able to work quickly, so have everything ready before you start. The contents of the two pots have to reach the right temperature — 150°C — at the same time. To be sure, it is best to use a candy thermometer.

pistachio, saffron and honey torrone

edible rice paper
⅓ cup liquid glucose
1 ⅓ cups caster sugar
½ cup water
⅓ cup honey
2 egg whites
2 pinches saffron, finely ground
1 teaspoon vanilla essence
150g pistachio nuts, toasted and chopped

Line a 15cm-square brownie tin with plastic wrap, leaving enough to cover the top later. Cut a square of rice paper to fit the base of the tin and place it in the base.

In one pot, put the liquid glucose, sugar and water and heat, stirring until sugar has dissolved. Increase the heat, brushing down any sugar that has stuck to the sides. Bring to the boil. The temperature needs to reach 150°C.

In a second pan, bring the honey to the boil. Again, the temperature needs to reach 150°C.

In a cake mixer, beat the egg whites until stiff peaks form. Continue beating and, in a thin stream, pour in the hot glucose and sugar syrup, then add the honey. Add the saffron and vanilla and beat until thick. Fold the pistachio nuts through and pour mixture into prepared tin. Cover with a sheet of rice paper and fold over the plastic wrap. Weight down and leave refrigerated for several hours until firm.

Cut into small squares. Wrap each square separately and store in refrigerator.

Note: I have tried to make this using manuka honey, but it did not work. I recommend you use a blended honey.

This is a classic torte. I first made a variation of this probably 20 years ago. It's great because it's easy to make and contains no flour. The yoghurt and date syrup is an optional extra for a special occasion.

dark chocolate, fig and almond torte with yoghurt and date syrup

6 large egg whites
225g caster sugar
200g 71 per cent chocolate, chopped
250g dried figs, sliced
150g toasted almonds, chopped
1 cup natural yoghurt and ½ cup date syrup to garnish (optional)

Set oven to 180ºC. Grease a 24cm springform tin.
   Beat the egg whites until stiff peaks form. Add sugar and continue to beat. Fold in the chocolate, figs and almonds.
   Pour into prepared tin and bake until golden brown on top.
   When ready to serve, pour over yoghurt and swirl with date syrup, which is available from speciality foodstores.

These Italian doughnuts are rapidly becoming a firm favourite in the Zarbo café where our bakers regularly make them on Saturdays.

bomboloni

Makes approximately 12

1½ teaspoons dry yeast
¼ cup warm milk
1 teaspoon sugar
1 cup plain flour
1 tablespoon sugar
1 egg
90g softened butter
grapeseed oil

to coat doughnuts

½ cup caster sugar
⅓ cup cinnamon

Place the yeast, milk and first measure of sugar into a bowl and cover. Set aside in a warm place to activate the yeast mixture for approximately 30 minutes.

In a food processor, process the yeast, flour, second measure of sugar and egg until well combined.

Add the butter a little at a time and pulse until it forms a soft, sticky dough.

Transfer to a clean bowl, cover and set aside in a warm place until mixture has doubled in size.

Punch dough and divide into balls about the size of 50-cent pieces and roll so they are round.

Leave in a warm place until they have doubled in size.

In a heavy-based saucepan, heat grapeseed oil and deep fry the balls of dough in batches until golden brown.

Once cooked, roll doughnuts in the sugar mix and insert the filling of your choice. It's best to insert the filling using a piping bag. You might like to try chocolate ganache, crème patissière or jam.

chocolate ganache

120g chocolate
100ml cream

Bring the cream to the boil, pour over the chocolate and stir until smooth. Allow to cool before use.

crème patissière

2 cups milk
1 teaspoon vanilla essence
4 egg yolks
½ cup sugar
⅓ cup cornflour

In a heavy-based saucepan, bring the milk and vanilla to the boil. Meanwhile whisk the remaining ingredients together until thick and pale. Pour one-third of the milk over the egg mixture and whisk well. Add the rest slowly while continuing to whisk.

Place mixture back into saucepan and stir over a low heat until thick. Allow to cool.

This is another popular item from the Zarbo bakery — the chocolate and Kahlua go together well.

chocolate kahlua slice

Makes approximately 18 slices

base

⅓ cup self-raising flour
¼ cup plain flour
2 tablespoons Dutch cocoa powder
⅓ cup caster sugar
1 egg
2 teaspoons vanilla extract
70g melted butter
¼ cup milk

topping

400g cream cheese
100g mascarpone
100g sour cream
⅓ cup caster sugar
3 eggs
1 shot espresso coffee
70ml Kahlua

Set the oven to 180ºC. Grease a 20 x 30 cm slice tin and line with baking paper.

To make the base, sift the flours and cocoa powder into a large bowl. Stir in the sugar. Add the egg, vanilla extract, melted butter and milk and stir until just combined. Spoon the mixture into the prepared slice tin and bake for 10 minutes. Allow to cool while you prepare the topping.

Turn the oven down to 160ºC.

To make the topping beat the cream cheese, mascarpone, sour cream and sugar in a mixer until smooth. Add eggs one at a time. Lastly fold in the coffee and Kahlua. Pour onto the base and bake for a further 30 minutes until set.

Here's another favourite from the Zarbo bakery. Using the basic recipe you can change the fruits and have a play.

peach and blackberry cake

Serves 8

185g butter
185g caster sugar
1 egg
1 egg yolk
335g plain flour
1 teaspoon baking powder
3 peaches, each cut into 8 pieces
200g blackberries
2 tablespoons caster sugar
icing sugar for dusting

Set oven to 180°C. Grease a 20cm springform tin.

Cream the butter and first measure of sugar together until pale. Add egg and yolk and beat well to combine. Mix in flour and baking powder to form a soft dough.

Roll out half the dough to fit the base of the prepared tin and line the base with the dough. Place the peaches, blackberries and remaining sugar over the dough. Roll out the rest of the dough and place on top of the fruit.

Bake until golden brown and set.

When ready to serve, sprinkle with a little icing sugar.

fig and plum tart

Serves 8–10

1 batch sweet short pastry (see below)
1 egg yolk
½ cup flour
½ cup sugar
1 teaspoon vanilla
1¼ cups cream
3 eggs
4 figs, halved
4 plums, halved and stone removed

Set oven to 170°C. Grease 23cm loose-bottom flan tin.

Roll out the sweet short pastry and line the base and sides of prepared tin. Blind bake the pastry by covering with tinfoil, taking care to push the foil down into the edges. Refrigerate for 15 to 20 minutes before baking for 8 minutes. Remove from the oven and prick the pastry, brush with egg yolk and return to the oven for 3 to 4 minutes until lightly golden.

Place flour, sugar and vanilla in a bowl. Add cream gradually, whisking to prevent lumps forming. Beat in the eggs one at a time, whisking after each addition.

Arrange the fruit on the prepared tart shell and pour over the batter.

Bake until golden, approximately 20 minutes.

sweet short pastry

200g butter, softened
150g icing sugar
2 eggs
400g plain flour, sifted

Cream butter and icing sugar together. Beat in eggs one at a time. Mix in the flour. Remove from the food processor or bowl and knead until well combined. Pat the dough into a ball and wrap in plastic. Refrigerate for 30 minutes before using.

New Zealand now makes some fabulous rosé wines and jellies are simple to make for a fun dessert. These jellies also look fantastic when made in wine glasses.

rosé and raspberry jelly

Serves 4

175g fresh or frozen raspberries
8 sheets gelatine
water, enough to just cover the sheets of gelatine
750ml rosé wine
125g caster sugar
raspberries to garnish

If you are using frozen berries, arrange them in a single layer on a couple of layers of paper towel to defrost. This drains excess juice from the berries.

Soak the gelatine in cold water for 3 minutes then squeeze.

Bring 200ml of the wine to the boil with the sugar, stirring until sugar has dissolved. Boil for 2 to 3 minutes. Add squeezed gelatine and stir until dissolved. Stir in the remaining wine.

Pour into four individual jelly moulds. Refrigerate for 1½ to 2 hours. Check after an hour to see how it is setting. Endeavour to reach the point where a raspberry dropped into the jelly will float suspended. At this point, divide the raspberries between the four moulds and refrigerate for several hours. To serve, run the moulds under a little warm water and invert onto individual plates.

Garnish with a few extra berries.

I first tried this sweet treat in Positano, on the Amalfi coast, and was intrigued by the combination. Serve with coffee, or with crème fraîche as a dessert.

melanzana dolce

Makes 64 pieces

1 very large eggplant, thinly sliced
flour for dusting
4 eggs, lightly beaten
grapeseed oil for frying
500g 70 per cent dark chocolate
75g hazelnuts, toasted and roughly chopped
100g glacé lemon peel, finely chopped
grated rind of 1 orange
½ teaspoon freshly ground nutmeg
½ teaspoon ground cinnamon

Lightly coat the eggplant with flour then with egg. Shallow fry in the grapeseed oil until lightly golden on both sides. Cook in small batches and drain on absorbent paper towel. Leave layered between paper to absorb as much of the oil as possible. Refrigerate for several hours or overnight.

Melt the chocolate over a double boiler.

Toss the chopped hazelnuts and the glacé lemon peel with the orange rind, nutmeg and cinnamon.

Line a 20 x 20cm tin with plastic wrap. Place one-third of the eggplant on the base. Pour one-third of the chocolate over the eggplant, sprinkle over half the nut and peel mix. Repeat the process with one-third eggplant, one-third chocolate and the remaining nut and peel mix. Place the remaining eggplant on top and pour over the remaining chocolate.

Refrigerate for several hours until set. Remove from the fridge, remove from the tin and remove the plastic wrap. Using a hot knife trim the edges until even and neat. Cut into 2.5 x 2.5cm squares.

Note: It is quite brittle, so cut gently.

These are both classic café cookies — try them at home.

mini almond crescents

Makes approximately 36

4 egg whites
500g ground almonds
475g caster sugar
zest of 2 lemons
½ teaspoon cinnamon
pinch of nutmeg
icing sugar for dusting

Set oven to 160°C. Place a sheet of greased and floured baking paper on a baking tray.

Beat egg whites until peaks form. Gently fold in other ingredients. Transfer the mix to a piping bag and pipe crescent shapes onto prepared tray. Bake 10 to 12 minutes until slightly browned. Cool on a wire rack.

Dust with icing sugar before serving.

chocolate pretzels

Makes approximately 36

250g butter
250g caster sugar
1 egg
1½ teaspoons vanilla
500g flour
125g Dutch cocoa powder
pinch of cinnamon
pinch of salt
egg white for glaze
a little dark chocolate, melted to decorate
a little white chocolate, grated to decorate

Beat the butter until smooth, add sugar and beat until light and fluffy. Beat in the egg and vanilla.

Sift the flour, cocoa, cinnamon and salt and blend in. Shape dough into a ball and wrap in plastic. Refrigerate for at least one hour.

Set oven to 180°C and place a sheet of baking paper on a baking tray.

Shape the dough into balls about the size of a 50-cent piece. Roll each ball into a rope, approximately 25cm long, and form into the shape of a pretzel. Place on baking tray and brush with beaten egg white and bake for 5 to 6 minutes until lightly browned. Allow to cool a little before transferring to a wire rack to cool.

When cool decorate with melted dark chocolate and sprinkle grated white chocolate over.

Some years ago the Zarbo bakers and I thought we'd have a bit of fun with one of our advertising campaigns. We decided to re-invent the toffee apple. We advertised on the radio as 'toffee apples — low fat, high energy'. We sold truckloads. This is one of those old-fashioned foods that the kids can help make.

Note: They are much easier to make with the help of a candy thermometer to check the temperature.

toffee apples

Makes 6 average-sized toffee apples

675g caster sugar
1 tablespoon white vinegar
1 tablespoon butter
65ml water
½ teaspoon cream of tartar
red food colouring (paste is best)
6 apples

Boil ingredients (apart from the apples) together without stirring until the hard-crack stage is reached (143ºC). Place the apples on skewers and dip into toffee mix. Allow to cool slightly and then roll in chips of coloured toffee.

coloured toffee

225g caster sugar
enough water to make a paste
  when added to sugar
food colouring (blue, green,
  orange, purple)

Boil sugar, water and chosen food colouring together until hard-crack stage is reached (143ºC). Pour onto a sheet of baking paper and allow to cool. Once cooled, break with a rolling pin.

This tart has a strong vanilla flavour that works well with berries. You can, however, make this tart with just about any fresh, soft fruit. If you can find them, try making it with old-fashioned, tart gooseberries.

Reserve the vanilla pods and put in an airtight container with 500g sugar to allow flavour to infuse sugar for later use.

mixed berry and vanilla tart

Serves 8

250g mascarpone
1 cup caster sugar
6 eggs
2 vanilla pods
2 tablespoons vanilla essence
28cm sweet pastry shell, blind baked (see fig and plum tart, page 154)
1 cup apricot jam
½ cup water
500g mixed berries

Set oven to 180°C.

Whisk the mascarpone and the sugar together until smooth. Add the eggs one at a time, beating well after each addition.

Split the vanilla pods in two and scrape out the seeds and add the seeds to the vanilla essence. Mix this through the mascarpone mixture. Pour into the prepared pastry shell.

Bake until filling sets, approximately 15 to 25 minutes. Remove from oven and allow to cool.

Place the jam and water in a saucepan and bring to the boil. Place the berries on top of the cooled tart and brush with the jam to glaze.

Semifreddo is the Italian word for 'half-cold' and is a chilled or partially frozen dessert. This variation on the theme is easy to make at home as an alternative to ice-cream.

chocolate semifreddo with semi-dried cherries

Serves 8–10

600ml thickened cream
2 eggs, separated
100g icing sugar
100g dark chocolate, roughly chopped
100g semi-dried cherries, chopped

Whisk the cream until it forms soft peaks. Beat the egg yolks and 25g of the icing sugar together until pale.

Whisk the egg whites until they form firm peaks. Gradually add the remaining sugar and whisk until stiff and glossy.

Fold the egg yolk mix through the cream, then fold through the egg whites. Finally fold through the chocolate and cherries.

Pour into a freezer-proof container and freeze for 24 hours. Leave to stand at room temperature before spooning into serving dishes.

Tequila is one of those alcohols we don't usually associate with baking, but try this as a summer dessert — the chilli sugar really sets it off. If you are making small tarts you will need more pastry.

tequila tart with chilli sugar

Makes 1 large or 10 small tarts

¼ cup cream, lightly whipped
1 cup sugar
6 eggs
½ cup tequila, heated, flamed and cooled
½ cup orange juice
28cm sweet pastry shell, blind baked (see fig and plum tart, page 154)

Set oven to 180ºC.

Mix the cream and sugar together. Add eggs one at a time mixing well after each addition. Finally, add the tequila and orange juice and mix well. Pour into prepared pastry shell and bake until filling is set, approximately 15 to 20 minutes. Set aside to cool.

When ready to serve, decorate with chilli sugar.

chilli sugar

1 cup sugar
water
1 chilli, seeds removed
1 teaspoon rock salt
zest of 1 lime

Combine the sugar and enough water together to form a thick paste. Bring to the boil and continue boiling until it turns a caramel colour. Pour onto a greased tray to set.

Break up and place in a food processor and pulse to form medium-fine granules.

Place the rest of the ingredients in a mortar and pestle and grind into a rough paste. Mix in the caramelised sugar.

Although I have made this with a selection of berries, you can use just about any seasonal fruit. Ripe stone fruits, or a selection of assorted pears are also delicious with a coriander sugar. If you use frozen berries allow to thaw on paper towels to absorb excess moisture.

autumn fruit salad with basil sugar

Serves 4

1 cup caster sugar
a little water
1½ cups red wine
4–8 pink peppercorns
2–3 cups fresh or frozen mixed berries,
  e.g. strawberries, blackberries, raspberries, blackcurrants and redcurrants
12 basil leaves
1 cup caster sugar

Place the first measure of sugar in a heavy-based saucepan with just enough water to make a thick paste. Gently heat until it just starts to turn a caramel colour and then add the red wine and pink peppercorns. Boil for 2 minutes and pour over the berries and allow to cool.

Pound the basil and the second measure of sugar in a mortar and pestle.

Place a mound of berries on individual serving plates and top with the basil sugar.

Traditionally tiramisu is made with coffee, but this is a white tiramisu made with berries and zabaglione. I like to make zabaglione with apple juice rather than the usual Marsala. To this I add grated white chocolate and mascarpone. The result is both rich and decadent.

white chocolate and berry tiramisu

Serves 6–8

4 tablespoons caster sugar
4 egg yolks
⅔ cup apple juice
100g crumbled white chocolate
250g mascarpone
1½ packets savoiardi biscuits
2 cups assorted mixed berries
extra white chocolate to garnish

Place the sugar and egg yolks in a non-reactive bowl and whisk to combine. Place over a double boiler and bring the water to the boil while constantly whisking the sugar and egg mix. Slowly add the apple juice and continue to whisk until thickened, approximately 15 minutes. Add the chocolate and whisk to melt. Finally add the mascarpone and whisk until combined.

Line the base of a baking tray with a layer of the biscuits. Cover with one-third of the zabaglione mixture and sprinkle over the berries.

Pour over another third of the zabaglione mixture and cover with another layer of the biscuits. Pour over the remaining zabaglione mixture.

Top with extra shaved white chocolate and refrigerate for several hours before serving.

It's hard to find the juicy pears that I remember from my childhood. The ones in the stores are nowhere near as juicy as I remember. However, poaching pears takes them to another dimension. In this recipe the cooled, poached pears are wrapped in filo and baked.
The light papery texture of the filo works well with the soft sweetness of the pear.

baked pears

Serves 4

500g sugar
500ml water
100ml whisky
4 pears, cored and peeled, stems retained
100g hazelnuts, toasted, skinned and finely chopped
100ml chocolate ganache (see bomboloni, page 148)
16 sheets filo pastry
100g melted butter

Bring the sugar, water and whisky to the boil. Reduce the heat and place the pears into the syrup. Cover and simmer until cooked. Remove from the pot and refrigerate until cold.

Mix hazelnuts and ganache together and place in a piping bag.

Once the pears are cold remove from the fridge and pat   with a paper towel. Pipe the hazelnut mix into the core.

Set oven to 200°C. Grease a baking tray.

Lay four sheets of filo out and brush with butter between each layer. Place a pear in the centre of the pastry and wrap to form a parcel. Repeat three times, placing each pear parcel on the baking tray.

Bake until crisp and golden, approximately 15 to 20 minutes.